A

FLOWER

FROM

MARS

A FLOWER FROM MARS

Kianah Rene

Black Castle Media Group, Inc.

Black Castle Media Group books may be purchased for

educational, business, or sales promotional use.

For information, please email

contact@blackcastlemediagroup.com

www.blackcastlemediagroup.com

First Edition

Cover Design by: Indestructible Minds

Library of Congress Cataloging-in-Publication Data

has been applied for.

Paperback Edition   ISBN: 979-8-9902391-9-7

Kindle Edition   ISBN: 979-8-9902391-8-0

EPub Edition   ISBN: 979-8-9902391-7-3

ECHOES

OF

INNER

WORLDS

In the labyrinth of my thoughts,
I wander
Sometimes lost in a storm.
Yet, I'm learning to love this intricate brain
of mine.
To know beauty in the midst of rain.
To know joy in the midst of pain.
For each thought
a star in the night sky
some dim, some bright
some just passing by.
In this galaxy, I've learned to find peace
embracing the constellations
that shape my space.

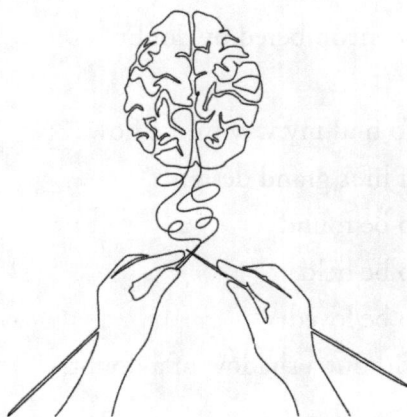

Oh, how I yearn for a connection
that is genuine.
Where understanding flows freely
unencumbered by doubt.

To find my way in the flow
of life's grand design
to be found
to be held
to be loved
without a shadow of a doubt.

So I wander
lost but with hope in my heart.

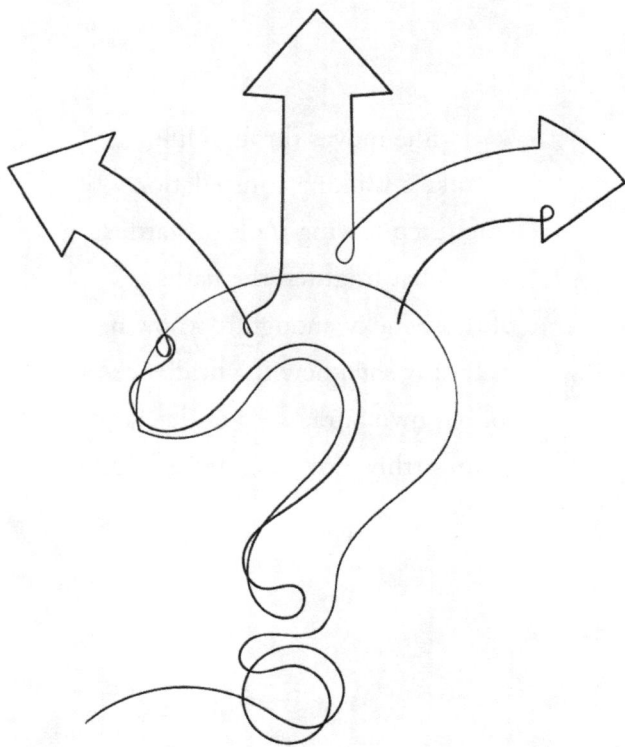

She moves through life
like a walking constellation
each step leaving trails of stardust
that brighten the paths
of those lucky enough to know her.
If only she knew the brilliance
of her own aura, she'd understand
the unearthly glow she carries within.

A Flower From Mars

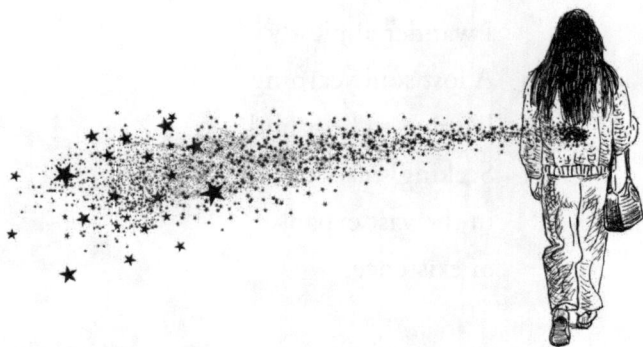

In the depths of my soul
I wander aimlessly
A lost soul yearning,
longing to be found.
Seeking solace
in the vast expanse
of existence.

Words escape my lips,
but they fall on deaf ears,
Lost in translation,
lost in the void of indifference.
I crave for someone
who speaks the same language
as me
Whose understanding brings
comfort like a blanket on a
cold day.

Fear of hurt is this shadow we let follow
but within that darkness
lies the potential
for a sunrise of strength.
It's the hesitant step
before a dance with vulnerability
where the fear of pain
may obscure the beauty of resilience

waiting to unfold.

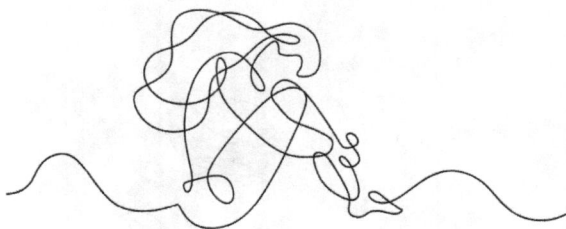

The fear of outgrowing
someone you love
is like holding
onto a rose
hesitant to bloom
unaware that in letting go
you both might discover
gardens within yourselves.

Discovering that someone
who feels like home
can also be harmful
is like realizing your sanctuary
is built on shifting sands;
a poignant reminder
that not all homes are safe havens
and some familiar doors
may lead to storms
instead of shelter.

A broken heart is a silent cry for the love that's lost.

In the end, it's the memories of love that can hurt the most.

Memories like stars
scattered across time.
Each one a story,
in the constellations
of our mind.

Within the shadow of his expectations
she stands
A desperate child
seeking his guiding hand.
Always yearning for his nod of approval
But feeling as if it never ends.
She wears her achievements like armor
Hoping one day
she'd finally belong.
But his standards
loom like an endless chase
A relentless journey
to an undefined place.

She's been a seeker
for quite some time
A silent approval
like a mountain to climb.
Every endeavor
an attempt to be seen
But his *well done* remains in between.
Like a phantom it haunts her dreams
She continues until she finds her worth,

A place where she belongs.

Hands outstretched searching
for a perfect fit.
Longing for the touch
that sets my heart on fire.
A gentle graze
a tender embrace
a simple gesture
To bridge the gap to illuminate
life's mysterious maze.

In this realm of uncertainty
and disarray, I seek refuge
a sanctuary
within a compassionate soul.
To be seen, to be heard
to be understood.

To find peace
in another's hold,
to feel whole.

My heart whispers words
meant only for you,
trapped inside unsent letters.

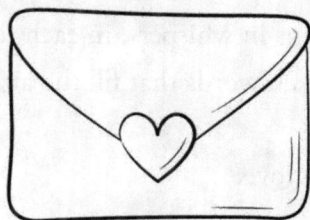

In the stillness of night
I found a love without a single sound.
A quiet love, like morning's hush
It blooms in whispers, in each touch.
Unspoken words that fill the air

A silent love.

It's in the spaces between our sighs
where a love unspoken truly lies.

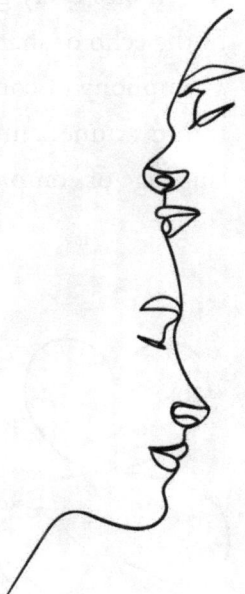

In the intertwining of minds,
a silent conversation blooms,
A dance of thoughts, understanding
woven into every glance.
In the echo of shared thoughts,
a symphony of connection,
Hearts attuned, finding solace in the
language of comprehension.

A love awakening within my chest,
A feeling that can't seem to rest.
It's like a storm and a gentle breeze,
A love that puts my heart at ease.
In the deepest chambers of my soul,
This love has taken full control.
It's something new, an unknown art,
sketched into my soul.

She's a garden of beauty,
blooming in humble unawareness.
If only she could see
the flowers of joy she plants
in every heart around her
she'd understand the wonder that is

her.

She's an unsung melody
in a crowded world
unaware of the sweet music she brings.
If only she knew the notes
of her own beauty
the world would stand still to listen.

Kianah Rene

In the garden of emotions,
I am a rose with thorns
guarding my fragility.
Though my petals long
for loves touch and comfort
my thorns keep them at a far.
A testament to the paradox of
desiring warmth while fearing
the vulnerability it brings.

Words unspoken,
linger in the silence
Emotions run deep
like a language of defiance.

Sometimes
my heart whispers fears
the mind can't comprehend
and I'm left with that pit
in my stomach
a cryptic reminder
of untold emotions.

A pit in my stomach dancing to the
rhythm of the inexplicable.

In the midst of us
echoes of the past arise
Moments, words,
begin to rekindle
the old ties.
Triggers whisper stories
we've yet to mend
But together, we'll find
healing in the end.

Fear of love
is like standing
at the edge of a vast ocean
afraid that its depths
might engulf us.
Yet, within that fear
lies the potential
for a breathtaking journey
where the waves
of vulnerability
carry us to shores
we never dared to explore.

In a world where trust can crumble like sand,
She guarded her heart with a cautious hand.
Past betrayals left scars, etched deep within,
A mural of hurt, where trust had been painted.

But in the dark soil of her wounded soul,
A seed of hope had been planted.
She watered it with tears, with tender care,
For trust, she learned, was not far from repair.

With time and patience, walls began to fade,
And slowly, She let trust's light flow.
In vulnerability, she found her way,
To heal the wounds, and let love stay.

No longer a prisoner of doubt's hold,
She now let trust bloom in an open space.
For in the tender petals of trust's flower,
She found the strength to heal.

In the reflection of her eyes
I see a hunger for more
a longing for a love grander than before.
I vow to be the architect of that "more,"
sculpting a love that screams her worth
a song of affection
where every note resonates
with the promise of giving her the abundance
she deserves

I have it.

Don't give up on me.

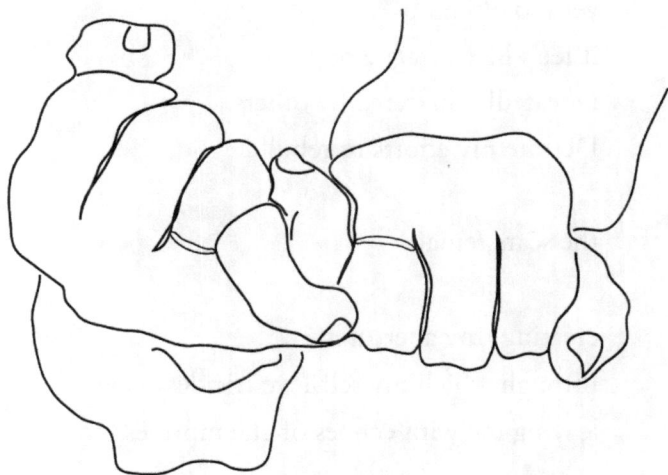

In the delicate chambers of my heart
self-love is a precious elixir
yet too often
it feels like a fragile box
repeatedly shattered by others.
Despite my efforts to rebuild

the scars remain

creating tiny apertures
through which my self-love trickles away
leaving me with echoes of an emptiness

I strive to fill.

The saddest words
are the ones left unspoken
in the name of love.

Love's wounds can cut deeper
than any blade.

In the caverns of my heart
emotions ruminate,
too intense,
stories I feared to tell.
A master at concealing
I played the part
Shoving them down
hiding my art.

Yet, beneath the surface,
a cauldron simmered,
feelings suppressed.
A boiling point,
an eruption near,
Until I learned
to shed my fears.

Now, I'm unraveling the layers
one by one
Inviting others to witness
the battles won.
No longer confined, emotions free
A dance with vulnerability.

I'm letting others glimpse the stormy sea,
finding peace in shared humanity.
For in the openness, a healing begins,
As I learn to let emotions live.

In this whirlwind of my emotions
I find
I've lost control
there's turmoil in my mind.
Pushing away the one
who holds my heart
I see the fractures
the chasms start.

Yet, within this chaos
a vow I make
To mend the bonds for love's sweet sake.
I'll gain control
rein in the storm
A metamorphosis a heart reborn.

For in this turbulence
a seed is planted
A promise to heal what's been overthrown.
To be better, for me, for her
to find love's sanctuary
in the calm of my mind.

The quiet whispers of her longing,
she yearns to be my shelter, my refuge.
Unaware that within the embrace
of her smile,
I've found the sanctuary my heart craves.

She dreams of being the haven in my storm,
a lighthouse to guide me through the night.
Little does she know, in her laughter,
I've found the warmth of home's soft light.

Her love is a harbor, sought and imagined,
yet she doesn't realize, in her mere existence,
I've already anchored my heart, secure,
and found my haven in her.

In the gallery of my thoughts
she yearns to decipher the abstract strokes
while I, with hesitant brushstrokes
paint doorways for her to wander within.
Together, we navigate
the masterpiece of my mind
transforming curiosity into an art
of understanding.

Her patience
is a gentle breeze
that caresses the wounds within
as she delicately
unravels the layers of my pain.
In her understanding
she doesn't offer a cure
but becomes the healing presence
a true companion
in the process of stitching
the fragments of my heart
back together.

I discovered a love
that transcends words
a language written
in the silent poetry of shared glances
and gentle touches.
She showed me a love I never knew existed
and now
I can't imagine a world without it.

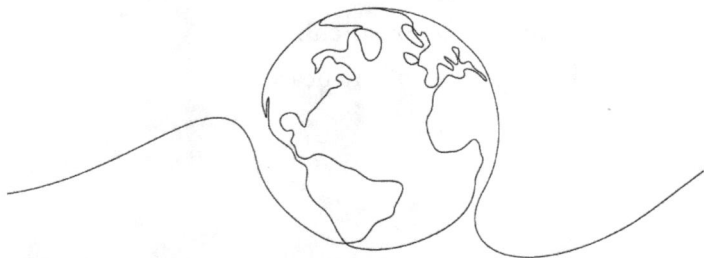

Her sweetness
is a taste of joy
that lingers on my lips.
Loving her
is like indulging
in the sweetest candy.
Each moment
a delicious treat
that leaves me
craving more.

I crave mastery of the emotional tides
inside of me.

I find myself adrift
in the sea of misunderstanding.

the silent struggle

written in the language
of unspoken desires.

In the art of self-mastery
emotions are the colors
and I am the artist
learning to create a masterpiece
from the palette of

my mind

and

my soul.

Within the twilight of youth,
the idea of growing up
looms like uncharted territory.
Fear shouts in the corridors of change,
yet within this uncertainty lies
a canvas for transformation,
waiting to be painted
by the colorful strokes of self-discovery.

Healing is not about erasing the past
but creating a present
where wounds
                    no longer dictate the rhythm
                                of our hearts

and love becomes the soothing balm
that orchestrates our new beginning.

Life's journey is not measured
by the miles we travel
but by the love we share
the scars we mend
and the beauty we find
in the midst of chaos.

Not succumbing to shadows,
I found strength within,
Surviving my own storm,
a story of resilience.
Now I stand with gratitude,
embracing light,
Learning to love and live,
through day and through
night.

Embracing our scars,
a testament to our past,
The reminder that we are meant to last.

Amidst the winter's chill,
with my soulmate near,
An oasis in their arms,
all doubts disappear.
Like a cozy hearth,
their love blankets around,
In the cold night's embrace,
warmth is found.

Embrace the storm
the thunder's roar
For in its chaos
there is love.
Through raindrops
you'll find a hidden serenity
A path to life's warmth.

In your eyes,
I witness the warm embrace
of eternity
As time fades away
leaving only you and I.

Within your gaze
forever finds its ideal space
With you
I know my heart is safe.

In the cold of night, we find our warm retreat,
Wrapped in love's embrace, our hearts skip a beat.
Amidst the chill, our souls' warmth takes flight,
Together, we kindle the fires of endless night.

In your laughter
I find a melody of joy

just you and me

In your eyes, I found my
favorite constellation.

In your smile,
I see the promise of
tomorrow.

In your eyes,
I see the reflection of
my soul.

Like morning sun on fields of green,
   You're the loveliest sight I've ever seen.

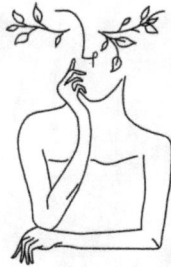

In her soul's gaze, a universe I find,
Eyes that hold galaxies, a love undefined.
In her understanding, my essence sings,
Together, a symphony of beautiful things.

In the depths of despair
I glimpsed a world unnoticed
The beauty in the humdrum
in every blade of green.
A heart that learned to heal
found love in life's grasp
Grateful for each moment
and the beauty of this space.

Trust the whispers
of your intuition;
it holds the wisdom
of a thousand choices.
You have a garden
of self-belief
it grows the certainty
that your instincts
know the way.

In the symphony of life
trust yourself
to be the conductor
of your own melody.
Each note played with
confidence is a step
towards the masterpiece
only you can compose.

In her eyes
the universe unfolds
yet she remains oblivious
to the galaxies she carries within.
She's a masterpiece
painting colors in every life she touches
blissfully unaware
of the masterpiece she is herself.

Like a compass points to the North Star,
my heart always finds its way to you.

Love is not just a feeling; it's the art
of choosing each other every day.

Love is the language of the heart, and
you are my favorite conversation.

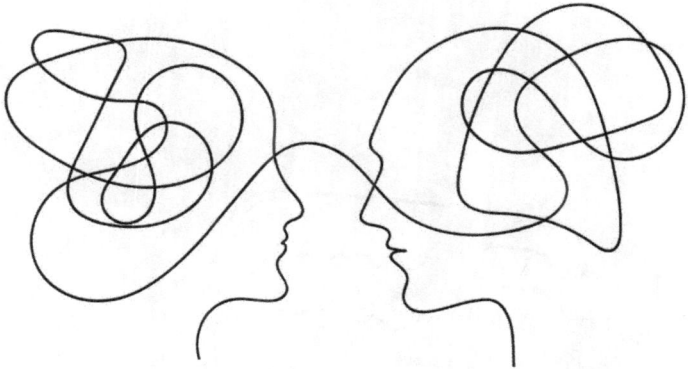

With you
every day is a love letter
waiting to be opened.

In your presence
time seems to disappear.

Someone I'd watch through
countless days and years.

Forever lost in your eyes
a timeless view.

With every glance
my love for you renews.

In your eyes
I see a universe of love
waiting to be explored.

To be seen,
is like having your soul's whispers
acknowledged,
a rare recognition that screams in the heart,
illuminating the beauty
of being truly known.

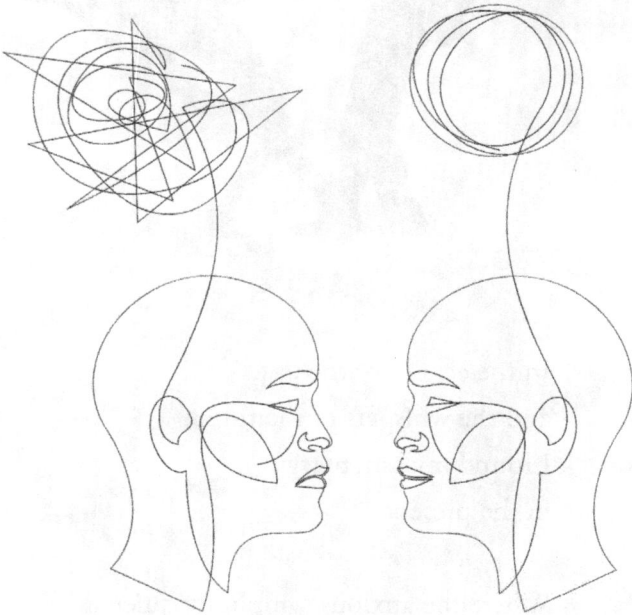

In the echoes of the past
and the whispers of the future
I found my sanctuary
in the present.

Where the anxious symphony quieted
and the melody of now
became the song of peace.

While I danced
with the ghosts of yesterday
and the shadows of tomorrow.

I stumbled upon the comfort of today.

Embracing the present
I found my escape to calm.

Where anxiety whispered its last
and peace became the dance partner
I never knew I needed.

Like flowers
to the sun
my heart turns to you.

With you,
even the ordinary
becomes extraordinary.

In your love
I am both lost and found.

Your touch is the language
my soul always understood.
In your embrace, I found the
warmth my heart always craved.

Realizing your worth
feels like unearthing a rare gem
within yourself.

a luminous discovery
that transforms the ordinary stones
of self-doubt into precious jewels
of self-love.

Insecurity is the subtle art
of underestimating
the kaleidoscope within
painting ourselves in hues
too dim to capture
the vibrant spectrum
we truly are.

In the present moment,
we find our roots entwined
with the essence of nature.
Like trees standing tall,
we learn the beauty of being
anchored in the now,
branches reaching for the sky
while grounded by the soil
that is now.

A mastery of thoughts,
I freed myself
from the shackles of the past
and the chains of the future.
Embracing the profound importance
of now,
I became the architect
of my safe haven,
sculpting each moment
with a taste of presence.

We are now.

Healing is the gentle rain
that nurtures the soul's wounded garden.

In the silence of the night,
I sip the sweetness of life,
A taste like milk and honey.

Sunsets whisper secrets
dusk's gentle plea
a fading light, we find ease.

In the art of acceptance
I released the need
for others to fit the canvas
of my expectations.

Like colors blending effortlessly
I found beauty in embracing them for
who they are
not who I wished them to be
a masterpiece of authenticity

painted with the strokes of understanding.

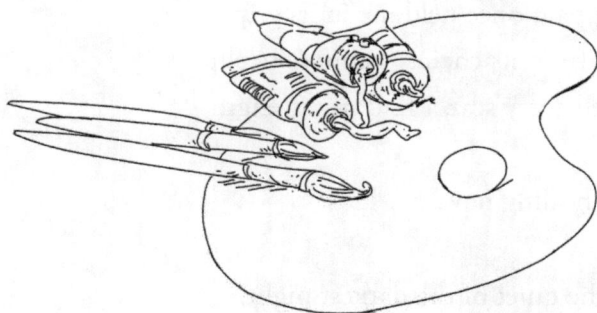

Beneath my scars, a tapestry unfolds,
Invisible threads of stories never told.
I've stitched my wounds
with threads of hope,
Healing's slow climb.

The pain once held me in its grip,
But from its chains, I choose to slip.
With every scar, I find my strength,

I'm healing now.

In the quiet of the darkest night,
I whispered to the stars.
And as the dawn began to steal,
I found the salve that helped me heal.

It's your turn now...

YOUR

INNER

WORLD

What is something you wish you could tell
your younger self?

_____
_____
_____
_____
_____
_____
_____
_____
_____
_____
_____
_____
_____
_____
_____
_____
_____
_____

Think of your favorite person, what makes them so special to you?

_____

_____

_____

_____

_____

_____

_____

_____

_____

_____

_____

_____

_____

_____

_____

_____

_____

Write a love poem to yourself...

_____

_____

_____

_____

_____

_____

_____

_____

_____

_____

_____

_____

_____

_____

_____

_____

_____

_____

If someone could walk a physical path through your mind, describe what that would look like?

_____

_____

_____

_____

_____

_____

_____

_____

_____

_____

_____

_____

_____

_____

_____

_____

_____

_____

_____

We all have things we are afraid we will never be healed of. Write it down to take away it's power.

_____

_____

_____

_____

_____

_____

_____

_____

_____

_____

_____

_____

_____

_____

_____

_____

_____

_____

How do you feel?

_____

_____

_____

_____

_____

_____

_____

_____

_____

_____

_____

_____

_____

_____

_____

_____

_____

_____

_____

Kianah Rene

THANK
YOU

ACKNOWLEDGMENTS

I am deeply grateful to everyone who has contributed to the
creation of my first poetry book,
"A Flower From Mars."
It has been a journey filled with inspiration,
reflection, and growth, and I am so lucky to have had the
support and encouragement
I received along the way.

First and foremost, I would like to express my
heartfelt appreciation to my family for their support and
encouragement. Your belief in me has been an anchor
through the highs and lows of this creative endeavor.

To my partner, thank you for being my rock and
for always cheering me on, even when
the words seemed to elude me.
Words could never explain how lucky I was to have you by
my side through this process. Lucky me.

A special thank you to my friends and fellow writers who
have offered invaluable guidance, constructive feedback,
and endless inspiration. Your wisdom has shaped this in
profound ways, and I am forever grateful.

I extend my gratitude to the team at Black Castle Media Group whose dedication and expertise have transformed my vision into a reality.

To Mr. Amari Soul, your passion for literature and commitment to excellence have made this journey an enriching experience. Thank you.

To my readers, thank you for embarking on this journey with me. If we weren't friends before, we are now.

Your support and encouragement mean the world to me, and I hope that my words resonate with you in ways that inspire, uplift, and evoke thought.

I hope even just one of you feel understood or seen.

Lastly, I dedicate this book to anyone who has ever doubted life, dared to dream, to feel, and to express themselves through the power of poetry. May these words serve as a reminder that our voices matter, our stories are worth telling, and our hearts have the power to touch the world.

With nothing but love,

Kianah Rene

Printed in the USA
CPSIA information can be obtained
at www.ICGtesting.com
LVHW092016130624
782911LV00010B/861

9 798990 239197